Snack Attack

Jan Burchett and Sara Vogler

Houghton Mifflin Harcourt.

MW00964805

Snack Attack was originally published in English in 2016. This edition is published by arrangement with Oxford University Press.

U.S. Edition copyright © 2019 by Houghton Mifflin Harcourt Publishing Company
Text and illustrations © Oxford University Press 2016

All rights reserved. No part of this work may be reproduced or transmitted in any form or by any means, electronic or mechanical, including photocopying or recording, or by any information storage or retrieval system, without the prior written permission of the original copyright owner identified herein, unless such copying is expressly permittedby federal copyright law.

Printed in China

ISBN 978-0-358-26185-8

1 2 3 4 5 6 7 8 9 10   XXXX   28 27 26 25 24 23 22 21 20 19

4500000000   A B C D E F G

Text © Jan Burchett and Sara Vogler 2016
Illustrations © Sarah Horne 2016
Inside cover notes written by Karra McFarlane

Acknowledgments

Series Editor: Nikki Gamble

The publisher would like to thank the following for permission to reproduce photographs: **Cover and p12:** Studio 8 Ltd; All other photographs provided by Shutterstock.

Houghton Mifflin Harcourt Publishing Company
125 High Street
Boston, MA 02110
www.hmhco.com

Contents

The Market

I am Pat and this is Ted.
We are going to
make snacks.

We get food that is good for us at a farmer's market.

I need food to run and kick!

Cook

This is how to make the snacks.

1. Boil six eggs.

Eggs can make me strong.

6

2. Peel the shells off the eggs.

3. Mash three of the eggs with a fork.

4. Cut up three of them.

Chop

5. Peel the carrots and grate them.

6. Chop up the melon and red pepper.

7. Chop up all the rest.

8. Make lots of toast.

The Snacks!

9. Now, finish the snacks.

   Put on the eggs.

   Put on carrot and sweetcorn for hair.

   Put on pepper and melon for lips.

11

Make a Snack

Now you can make a snack!

carrot

melon

pepper

egg

toast